Remembering Everything

Derek Zanetti

ISBN-10:1515079015
ISBN-13:9781515079019

DEDICATION
To Christopher, My brother
(the only other survivor of the madness)

I would like also like to thank Matt Ussia, Tom Cox, J. Jones, and anyone else who encouraged me to continue with this second book.

CONTENTS

Introduction

All day long, everyday, things are happening all around you, both close and far away. Things are happening to you, and inside of you, and because of you, and in spite of you. Sometimes there is no way to control the things that happen to you. Sometimes, even when you can control the things that happen to you, they still don't turn out the way you think that they should.

Some people spend their entire lives trying to forget the bad things that have happened to them. They take those memories and try to black them out. They only want to remember the good memories, the Christmas mornings, the birthday parties, the home runs, the free breakfast buffets, or the time they had sex at summer camp under the docks. But life is more than just the good times you have. Certainly the good times happen and exist, but so do bad times, and boring times, and lazy times, and painful times, and everything in between.

I want to remember it all, and not forget the weird, bad, scary, painful, harsh times. And not just so that I can learn from them as a hope to not have them again, because even if you try as hard as you want to avoid it, the rain falls on everyone. But I try and remember what my mind felt like before experiencing such events.

Fear does odd things to your mind, so does pain and anxiety. Can you remember what it was like before you ever had a broken heart . . . have you ever tried?

Advice from Unknown Whales

When I was 17 years old, I took the money I had been saving, and I went on a trip to Maui, Hawaii. The plane ride was a long one. We stopped in LAX.

I was with other people, none of which were my family.

I may as well just had been alone.

Upon exiting the aircraft, we were greeted by women in grass skirts.

Their skin was very tan.

They put braided grass ropes around our necks.

My hair was bleach blonde; it was the 90's.

I was interested in a girl, who was on that trip. She's an adult now.

I ate pineapple on my pizza for the first time. I also ate sushi for the first time.

I was short and chubby, not much has changed.

I remember the weather. It was perfect. No humidity, it was always sunny.

I remember swimming in the ocean with my shirt on. I regret that now.

Not the swimming part, just the fact that I wasn't comfortable with myself enough to let my skin see the sunlight. I was hiding something.

I rented snorkeling equipment with a coupon I ripped out of a free paper advertisement.

I remember applying sunscreen to my neck and my arms and feet and legs.

I didn't put any on my face, because you don't really need it on your face when you're facedown snorkeling.

I tried to listen for whales communicating with one another.

I know I heard something; I'm not quite sure what it was.

I like to think that the whales were singing to each other.

I like to think that one day the words of their songs will subliminally come to me, and I'll be able to know what they were saying.

I went out pretty far. The water was so clear, I could see all the way to the bottom of the ocean floor.

The sun was shining brightly.

There were fish and turtles and water snakes and other swimming things.

It was beautiful. It was perfect. I remember it very well.

I saw a giant tree in the water. It frightened me in a very real way.

I panicked and quickly turned around, a wave came over my snorkel hole, and I breathed in a breathful of saltwater.

I choked, and coughed, and almost died.

I returned to shore and took off my shirt. My throat was sore from breathing in the saltwater. I'm sure you know the feeling.

The rest of the trip was fine, we went out and saw the fire eaters, and the hula dancers.

I ate plenty of delicious fruit, drank delicious coffee, and even bought a few puka shell necklaces.

I'm trying to remember what the whales told me while my head was submerged in the ocean, maybe it was something about swimming with my shirt off, maybe it was something about being true to myself. I'm trying to remember. I'm trying to remember.

We are All on a Road to Somewhere

We have all arrived here today, at the exact time we were
supposed to.

In our own different ways we are all taking a very
different mode of transportation,

that we ourselves took no responsibility for.

Some came by truck, some by car, a handful of
motorcycles, and a fair amount of SUVs,

and a remarkable amount of hybrid cars, driven mostly
by white people with too much time on their hands,
too much college debt, and NPR bumper stickers.

Everyone goes into different directions for very different
reasons.

Some people are moving towards something, and some
are just trying to get away.

Some people are going to a job they love.

Some people are leaving a house they can't stand.

Some people drive along this highway all by themselves
for their whole lives.

Some people have as many kids as they can,

And try to fit them into some mid-sized minivan,

Like puzzle pieces,

Like some Tetris video game,

Like caskets in a graveyard,

Like sardines in a can,

Like Twinkies in a box.

You see a lot of bumper stickers out here, some political, some just for kicks.

The thing about traffic is that it always exists somewhere.

9 AM rush hour,

5 PM rush hour,

Before the ball game starts,

After the ball game lets out,

Before the weekend,

After the weekend,

Friday fish fry at the VFW that doesn't have a parking lot,

At 4:30 in the morning when the first shift is getting ready to start,

At 8:30 at night when the Mormons gather at the root beer stand,

At 2 in the afternoon when the housewives of Upper Saint Clair emerge from their vodka bottles and sleeping pills to eat a $16 salad at some outdoor café in a shopping district in a neighborhood that is as unfamiliar to them as the words "sacrifice," or "contentment."

Everyone's coming and going. All day long, day after day from before you were born until you check outta here.

You can either choose to keep on driving up and down these highways or join the 20 car pile up just out side the Squirrel Hill Tunnel, where a mini-van covered in pro-life bumper stickers filled with more kids than seat belts got T-boned by the Upper Saint Clair house wife too drunk to drive, too sad to smile, and too bored to just stay at home.

The two cars danced their way under a flat bed truck that slid into a pair of 4x4 pick ups that smashed an SUV, that rolled into a flock of bikers, that wound up thrown all over three hybrid cars that all seemed to be in a row, like a domino set, like at some auto auction, like they where supposed to be there. The smoke rose like the Fourth of July, two cars had just caught fire, all the kids in the minivan were dead, most of the bikers died, the trucker escaped without a scratch, the drunken house wife took her dignity, and fled the scene. The hybrid cars began to melt like ice cream cones from the flames of the adjacent fires. NPR was playing over the radio. I sat there with my banjo and wrote a brand new national anthem.

After We Die

I was thinking out loud to myself for the last 31 years
About what happens after we die
And I didn't come up with any answers
I think about what it was like before I was born
And I can't remember anything
Other than the quiet blackness
Maybe we just return to the giant emptiness
Maybe we float naked in the black nothingness, silent
Maybe that's what will happen after we all die
Nothing
Just return to the quiet blackness
Just like it was before we got here
Maybe there won't be any memory to speak of
Just still and quiet and black
Like the first few moments we fall asleep, before
    dreaming starts
Or the nights we don't dream at all
Sometimes I think we think too much about it
Maybe it's not that complex
Maybe it's just black nothingness

I'm Not Afraid to Die

I'm not afraid to die anymore,

Not even a little bit.

I was thinking about growing old in a rocking chair somewhere,

And that sounded great.

With all white New Balance sneakers, and elastic banded khaki pants, a polo golf shirt from the local union hall, and some crusty old trucker hat.

And then for a second, I thought that maybe I'll get hit by a bus crossing the street in front of a coffee shop for all the onlookers to see, with blood running from my ears and nose.

And then, I thought about dying in my sleep next to my wife at the age of 37 of a brain aneurism, with all the peace and quiet surrounding me.

I had a thought that maybe I'd try to be the hero in some western style shootout and jump in front of a bullet meant for someone who is afraid of death.

In anyway, death is going to happen.

With or without your permission or consent.

I won't bear a grudge or feel cheated when I go.

I won't feel cut short or look back and wish things had been different for me.

I did it, I was alive.

I really felt things, with my skin, and with my heart.

I hope that the possessions I leave are few and not envied to be sold or stolen.

Carry on as you have, and be kind to one another.

All I ask is that you don't bury my body in the ground for people to see for the next 500 years.

I've tried to avoid living in the past while I was alive, and I sure as hell don't want to live in the past when I'm dead.

That's all a cemetery is, just another excuse to hold onto the past.

I'm ready to let go.

Cemetery Bullshit

All this land taken up by people who are gone,

like a breeze,

like dementia,

like regret.

There are more people being born everyday, but there's no more land being born for them to go to when they die.

It's unsustainable. It's ridiculous. It's selfish.

When I die feed me to the wolves,

bake me into a shepherd's pie for the cannibals,

drag me into the woods,

burn me in a pile,

use my skin for an umbrella,

turn my bones into jewelry,

make glue with my joints,

braid my hair for a rope swing,

boil my fat into organic soap like in Fight Club,

show my lungs to elementary school kids during an anti-cigarette campaign.

I won't be worried about what you're going to do,

because I'm dead,

just please don't bury me in a cemetery.

Because that's bullshit.

Skateboarding Nun

Somewhere south of Heaven, in between Earth and Purgatory is where all of the nuns that had premarital sex go to after they die. It's gray in color and smells of lemon scented floor cleaner. The outside parking lot is filled with moving trucks and broken down old air-conditioning units. Most of the nuns smoked their cigarettes all the way down past the filter, the other ones just ate a lot of candy like root beer barrels, salt water taffy, rock candy, Smarties, Necco Wafers, and mostly any other candy that had marshmallows in it. One day, I saw a few of them skateboarding down by the old docks. I think they may have noticed me watching off in the distance. They never said anything, but I could tell they didn't want me around.

Abortion Clinic Dream

I was just standing there, on the street corner with a small bag of popcorn and a small Cherry Coke watching the abortion protesters yelling and screaming and offering the love of Christ. There was a man with a megaphone on a small wooden box talking about the responsibility of others, inserting words like "salvation" and "repentance" and "sin." There were small children crying heavy tears, with rosary bead winter scarves, bleeding from their small cold faces, begging for their parents' approval. It was wintertime, the snow was falling, the slush from the streets seeped deeply into their shoes, and the glory of the lord was wrapped around them.

They brandished large Styrofoam signs adorned with dead babies and fictional statistics. I assumed most of them drove into town from the far outreaches of the rural conservative sects that kept them safe and secure. One man in a 20-gallon cowboy hat began burning the Constitution in a tin coffee can saying that homosexuality is destroying this country. He began to scream and cry for God to forgive us for the sins we have allowed our neighbors to commit. He looked a lot like a middle aged Tommy Lee Jones, but sounded like a southern used car salesman or a young George Bush Sr. At one point he threw himself onto the pavement and begged for God's mercy on this country. He apologized for the gays and lesbians, the abortionists and immigrants, and all the liberals who took prayer out of school, and the welfare culture that sent our country into financial ruin.

As I stood there, for what seemed to be an eternity, my anxiety was boiling over inside of me. I felt paralyzed. I felt helpless. I felt my teeth becoming loose in my Styrofoam head. I felt my brain swimming in an ocean between my ears. I heard Woody Guthrie calling my name. I saw a blood red film fall over everything in my peripheral. I felt alone and exhausted. I felt like it couldn't get any fucking worse.

And just then as I stood on the edge of the curb about to throw myself onto the black asphalt under an approaching bus, I saw them take a young girl who left the Planned Parenthood office and crucify her to the wood-grained paneling of a 1994 Dodge Caravan. They began throwing birth control pills and condoms at her as they chanted, "CRUCIFY! CRUCIFY! CRUCIFY!"

I just stood there on the curb, with my jaw wide open, popcorn spilling down the sewer drain, speechless. And then, I woke up. It was only 20 minutes after I fell asleep; I couldn't fall back asleep for the next few hours.

Newspaper Newspaper

I saw advertized in the newspaper that the IKEA by the airport is going to replace the welcome mat section with an abortion clinic. They wanted to insure you that no federal money will go into this new addition; it's all privately funded. They also are going to be offering hot air balloon rides, and free beer on the first Tuesday of the month (21+). The born again Christians are outraged but still buy the cheaply made furniture.

Three in One Day

From where we were staying on 3rd and 25th to where we were going 5th and 28th wasn't too far. We would eventually float there like ghosts. We stopped and got a coffee and a fruit cup at a corner store that looked like every other corner store in Manhattan (I drink a lot of coffee). We (Lindsey and I) walked and talked and ate and drank and laughed and people watched the few short blocks to get her to the studio she was working out of that day. The building was made out of black marble, it was so shiny that you can see your reflection in it (even though some people don't bother to check), and it smelled like the inside of a brand new car mixed with cardboard. I dropped her off by the front desk, gave her a kiss on her cheek exited the building, and turned right towards a self-serve coffee bar on the corner. I now had five hours to burn with only three writing assignments to tackle, which should be a breeze seeing as there are ten gallon tankards of Iced Hazelnut coffee in front of my face. All I need is a splash of iced coffee and a fist full of gummy bears, and I can write a novel (I've never written a novel).

I sit down, open my computer case, close my eyes, put on my headphones, turn the static all the way up, take three deep long breaths, open my eyes, and start writing. The writing assignment I had was pretty forgettable, a silly piece on a love triangle between a lawyer, a bartender, and a high school cheerleading coach. Most of the tables were taken, so I sat with my face to the window overlooking the bustling sidewalk at the store's front entrance, watching the passers by, pass by. On the far side of the side walk, about six feet from the front door of the café, was a middle-aged Indian man selling fruit, to the people walking in-between the busyness of their busy lives. He had an array of cardboard signs with prices written on them with black permanent marker (His penmanship was poor): Bananas 3 for $1.00, strawberries $2.00 a bucket, oranges 75 cents apiece, and so on and so forth. I first noticed him with his head down counting quarters into one-dollar stacks, as to give fast and accurate chance to his loyal regulars. Out of the corner of my eye through my dark-tinted Ray Ban sunglasses, I noticed the fruit stand man had 6 fingers on one hand, two thumbs to be exact. It was my first time ever seeing anything like it. The second thumb was active and very much a participatory member of the man's hand. It was a little smaller than the other but still functional. When I saw this it was almost 11:00 am.

I took a walk after lunch to Madison Square Park to find a shady spot to sit and think for a while. New York City is a busy place, and it's easy to just get lost in the great big shuffle of it all. So, I have always found it to be important to take time and just sit with my thoughts and try to sort them out the best I can. I always try to make a conscious effort to hold my head up instead of slouching (I have horrid posture), that way I can be aware of what's going on around me. I hear to my left a girl (about my age) crying about her failing relationship and that she had been cheated on many-many-many times within the last 6 months. I felt sad for her pain. She was truly, and deeply hurt. She was such a beautiful girl, smart and articulate. Her face had perfect symmetry. She was fit. She even had nice feet. I'm a sucker for nice feet, (I have caveman feet, hobbit feet, like a crusty red brick, like a smashed car at a junk yard, veiny, fat, they are always sweaty, they smell like shit, and no matter how hard I scrub them, they always look dirty and gross). I felt bad for her. Just then as I was thinking about her feet, I heard a loud crash, like lightning, like a home run ball being hit in a train tunnel, like a car accident, like Joe Theisman's shin bone, like the Fourth of July, like everyone one in the park all clapped their hands at the same time. I look over to my 11 o'clock and see that a tree branch has broken off of an enormous tree and fallen right onto the walkway where people were entering the park. You heard people shouting, some had fallen into the grass to avoid the large heavy branch. The thing that struck me the most was that the only person who was even close to the branch as it fell was a pregnant Asian woman in a pink dress. The people who shouted and threw themselves into the grass where in no danger at all of being hit by the falling branch. It was all just a show, perhaps a ploy to be noticed or gain sympathy. The only person almost hit by the branch was the pregnant woman, who wasn't much bothered or phased by it. Almost as if she saw it coming, or welcomed it, or hoped that it may have crushed her.

After that, I took a much longer walk to Thompson Square Park down past St. Mark's Place in the Lower East Side. I got a slice of pizza, and can of Cherry Pepsi, sat down and had either a late lunch or early supper. I actually prefer Coke to Pepsi, but I prefer Cherry Pepsi, to Cherry Coke. Not that either is any good for you or matters at all in the great scheme of things. It's just a stupid preference, but I guess most of life can be boiled down to that. I ordered one slice, extra cheese, extra mushrooms, extra napkins, which I ate on a park bench in the shade. Across from me were three men all talking to themselves. One was extra loud talking about business, one was whispering about love, and the other was trying to talk to his dead brother. His face was long and thin and painted with tears. They all looked empty and lonely and homeless and poor and sad. I felt bad for them. A horn of a bus or truck, or something larger than just a car horn, blew loudly. All three of the men lifted their heads to see what it was, when they realized it was nothing more than a horn, they all lowered their heads and continued their conversations with themselves. It was weird how the cigarette butts laid on the ground underneath them, like a cemetery, like students in a classroom, like church pews, like rush hour traffic.

I saw all three of these things in one day with my own eyes; I also decided to leave my phone in the room that morning, which makes me think a lot about everything else I usually miss.

Advice for You When You're Bored

Some people spend all day with their necks bent in half
thumbing on a screen talking to invisible people on an
invisible internet, on invisible wireless radio waves.

It's hard to notice anything when your head is always
bent to the ground.

You miss so much in the sky, to your left and to your
right.

It takes a lot away from your wonderment when
everything is at the tips of your constantly typing
fingers.

It does something to the child that lives inside of your
heart.

Maybe you're the kind who lets others to do your
dreaming and feeling for you. That certainly is a way
to live,

But if you feel things when your heart pumps blood to
your finger tips,

If you treasure moments when your hair stands up on the
back of your neck,

Try looking around.

The ends of your eyes can take in the glories and
wonders of everything, or nothing.

Take a drive to a place you've never been before, take a
look around, there's never a re-run, or a slow internet
connection when you can see something first hand
with your own eyes. Smells, and sights, and feelings
are going extinct. Enjoy them before it's illegal. I
think they are killing people in Missouri over it.

Cops

He said to me, "It's nothing personal. I just don't trust the cops."

Too many times you find someone lying there dead on the street, with blood in their mouth just as dead as can be. I saw a video on the computer once of the cops beating a homeless man to death because he didn't have nowhere to go. Of course he didn't have nowhere to go, he was homeless. He wasn't drinking or on any type of drugs or nothing. He was just sitting there, and the cops told him he had to go home. He tried to explain that he was on hard times, and he didn't have nowhere to go. I guess that was a good excuse as any to beat that poor man. The newspaper said he was slow or had a mental deficiency. Now, I had never met him or anything, but I do know it's a damn shame that they killed him.

You know that feeling in high school when somebody bigger and stronger and older than you wants to give you a hard time just because they can. They may follow you and call you names and make you feel small. They may spit at you or pull your hair, or try and take something that rightly belongs to you, all because they have the power over you to do it. That's how I feel when I see a cop. Even if you are doing the right thing, or in some cases not doing nothing at all, they can just come right up on ya and take what's yours. It's like being bullied. It's like being took. It's like you don't have anything to defend yourself with. Just because you may look different, they can just pull ya right on over and look through your things. Not that I have anything worth hiding, I just don't see it to be right that your private things can't be left private, ya know?

I heard they shot and killed that poor black boy over in Missouri, just for walking down the street. Just cause he was different, just cause they felt like it, and they knew they could get away with it. That don't seem right to me. That's something of evil. What kind of person do you have to be to always want to carry some gun on ya, trying to make everyone afraid. I don't know about you, but I certainly don't feel served or protected. I feel afraid, nervous, like they're out to get ya. Fear is a funny thing. It makes ya feel . . . afraid all the time, always looking over your shoulder, not really able to feel yourself. Eventually, people who are afraid get tired of being afraid, and they want to do something about it. They want to get out of it, ya know?

It's a real shame, I don't remember things being this way. You used to be able to speak your piece. You used to be able to stand up for something. Not only are you kept from doing that, they are just killing anything that moves, anything they feel shouldn't be moving. It's sad. I'm sure there are good cops still out there, but if there are, they sure ain't out helping the poor guys getting beat to death.

A Binary Poem About Two Different Types of Trainwrecks

Part 1

There's an ocean of plastic bags in my heart,
Sitting there stagnant, like Diaper Island,
Where all the six-pack holders with the dead fish go,
Where they buried Bigfoot after his body thawed.
Some garbage cans are filled with everything,
It's not certain we all get the same start,
Some start off with a lot more garbage than others.
Some are born wrapped in used flypaper, with piss warm
    Mt. Dew filled baby bottles and cigarette butt
    carpeted nursery floors,
Eating 3-day-old Spaghetti O's out of a can with a spoon
    used to scoop out wet cat food.
Newspapers stacked up on the stove, like some fire
    hazard Fourth of July daycare.
No grass in the backyard around the tree.
Broken windows stacked in the far north corner of the
    side yard, where kids are playing dangerously close in
    old flip flops 3 sizes too big, with very little hope of
    anything different,
A never corrected speech impediment that makes it
    nearly impossible to ever find future employment,
Over-weight, over-worked and drastically over-avoided.

Part 2

It's nice to have two parents and live in a quiet
    neighborhood,
With a backyard swimming pool, and nice kids around
    your age, whose parents are also still married,
To have American Eagle credit card grandparents,
That pay for your summer camp, and your shitty Denny's
    chicken finger meal,

Going to get braces, family vacations to the shore with
    the other rich families from the local country club.
Our dad is a real bad tipper: "Those people make enough
    money."
Season tickets to all the hockey games.
Every thing is so perfect, with a beautiful Christmas
    wreath collection,
Mom played piano when the other mothers are over,
    simply for jealousy's sake.
College was paid for.
Got a great job, in Dad's office, 401k, retirement, paid
    vacation, lemon slices in a pitcher of ice water.
So sure, so sure of everything.
It's nice to be sure.
Until one day you realize that every Monday morning
    when the trash man comes to take away your
    mountain of excess, leftovers, bullshit, and trash that
    it all has to go somewhere.
But where?
And then you're not so sure anymore.

Sandusky, Ohio

Everything was gray, and sounded like cardboard
The boys all have Justin Bieber haircuts
The girls all have Justin Bieber haircuts
The rain was so cold
The air smelled like Chelsea Clinton
I drank an Aquafina bottle full of gin
I urinated in a bush in the middle of Cedar Point
A man tried to confront me about urinating in the bush
I told him I was a veteran, and he shouldn't question me
I lied
I'm not a veteran
My feet were soaked from standing in a puddle
I took a seat next to an overweight youth
He was wearing a National LARPers Union hooded
    sweatshirt
It was his 30th time this year coming to Cedar Point by
    himself
I was drunk
So I was extra chatty
He said his parents drowned in one of the fountains in
    the food court last summer
I didn't ask any more questions.

Some People

Some People are waiting all week for the weekend

Some People are waiting all year for summer vacation, Christmas break, and tax returns

Some People are waiting their whole lives to be happy

Some People are dying to feel alive

Some People are working for someone else's dream

Some People are tying their own stomach in knots

Some People are praying for cancer

Some People are paying for war

Some People are diving into swimming pools filled with nothing

Some People are staving for a friend

Some People are begging for the wrong kind of change

Some People are never going to find it

Some People grow up, but everyone grows old.

Cats

If you have cats you shouldn't offer your home as a clean
   place to stay to people who are traveling

Cats poo and pee indoors

In a box

In the corner

In a pile of magical sand that's supposed to make it not
   stink

But it does stink

It stinks real bad sometimes

Moreover, their hair is everywhere

And it gets on your clothes

And makes you look stupid

Also, I'm allergic to cats

They make my eyes water

And my nose run

And they are very invasive

They don't hesitate to jump on your lap

Unwelcomed

And when you try to move them off they dig their claws
   into your jeans and put snags in your shirt

That really makes me mad

I fucking hate cats

I don't hate all cat owners, but it makes me question their
   integrity in regards to how they view the world
   around them

I can be your friend if you have cats, but I probably will
   never sleep over your house unless its wintertime,
   and I don't have any other options, but the whole time
   I will wish I was somewhere else.

27

Dairy Queen

I think that parents who take their kids to participate in beauty pageants should be forced to all live on the same island together. That way they only have to deal with people as arrogant and obnoxious as they are. If for one second you start to have hope for humanity, stay away from things like Pre-K cheerleading camps, any kind of middle school dance teams, or elementary school swimsuit competitions. I have never felt lower in my life than witnessing these people interact with one another. I've never wished such ill on any group of people. Not like death or anything, just like really bad acne breakouts, or stubbed toes, or that the group of them would all get a wad of bubblegum the size of a baseball matted into their hair. This is the story of something that I will never forget, this has stained my memory forever.

I got caught in a Dairy Queen one time, somewhere in Pennsylvania, and a troop of 6th grade choreographed dance competitors were there to have lunch on the way to some type of try out, or contest, or whatever. I would guess there were about 15 of them in number. I kept my sunglasses on the whole time, as I slowly ate my large Heath Bar Blizzard and large onion rings with about 20 packets of ketchup. I didn't approach them, I didn't ask any questions, I just sat there and watched. I am usually an outgoing fellow, at least outgoing enough to say hello, or maybe even ask what they were up to, but not this time.

As an outsider, I had no idea that dance troops traveled on a touring bus. I also had no idea that all, and I truly mean ALL of their mothers also attended. The prepubescent girls and their mothers alike all wore matching blue and white jump suits, with all white Nike trainers, and all had their hair up in a pony tail. I'm not sure, but I think that all of the girls and their mothers had the same haircuts. It looked cultish, but without the order and politeness of a cult. Most of the moms waited outside smoking cigarettes, and talking to one another about make up tips, and what is the best brand of clear coat to use to insure that your little girl's nail polish doesn't get scratched. Some of the mothers were very fit, and looked like they may have been cheerleaders themselves back in high school, and were looking to relive the glory days. Most of the other mothers certainly did not. They looked like Honey Boo Boo's Mother mixed with Jabba the Hut.

I had already ordered and was served my food, and thank God. If I had to wait in line and hear each one of the girls and their mothers order, I probably would have taken one of those long handled red Dairy Queen spoons and jammed them into my ear drums. I had my back to the far corner of the restaurant with my feet up on the bench seat. My head rested against the glass, and because I hadn't washed my hair in what very well could have been weeks, I left a giant grease smear on the window behind me.

The first girl and her mother approached the counter and began to order. "You go first Kristen," the mother said. Kristen began to order in the most slow motion fashion imaginable. "Ummmmmmmm... I think... I'll just have ummmmm . . . " (So far this part of the order took what seemed to be a week and a half.) She then gathered all her of wits about her and actually started to say food words, "The crispy chicken sandwich, no cheese, no lettuce, no onion, no tomato, just some ranch on the side, and an order of medium fries with cheese sauce on the side. And to drink I'll have —" Her mother (who looked like Violet Beauregarde's mother from Charlie and the Chocolate Factory) thin and tall and annoyed that she got fries with cheese says, "And a DIET Coke for her." The young girl (hoping to order a milkshake) looks at her mother with a sneer of frustration followed by a big pouty frown face. Her bottom lip was pushed so far out you could have parked a Buick on it. The mother rolled her eyes and chimed in and said, "I'll have the GRILLED chicken sandwich , NO bun, NO cheese, EXTRA vegetables, NO fries, and a Gatorade." The round faced, meek, brown-haired girl behind the counter very quietly and politely says, "Maam, we don't have Gatorade." The mother, who was not accustomed to disappointment, huffed and said loudly enough for all the other girls and mothers to hear, "I'll have a LARGE iced water, EXTRA lemon, EXTRA ice." You could see the eyes rolling in their heads from a mile away, knowing if they had ordered a Slurpee, or a milkshake, the shame that came along with it would be unbearable.

The line moved along order by order in a similar slow fashion. I just sat there, sunglasses on, trying my hardest to not have my head explode. Even when someone would order the double bacon cheeseburger with a large French fry, it would always be accompanied with a large water extra lemon extra ice or the only other acceptable choice, a Diet Coke, as to counter act the greasy burger and fry combo. The troop converged on the center table section, dragging the table and chairs together to make one long island of chatter, texting, and Diet Coke guzzling. I heard one of the thinner mothers say loud enough for everyone to hear, "I don't even remember what a French fry tastes like, I haven't had one since 1996." As some of the mothers nodded and nervously laughed, the others just shamefully shoveled in a mouthful of ketchup covered fries.

In total, the group was there for about 25- 30 minutes, but could easily had been mistaken for an eternity. Watching them eat reminded me of how seagulls behave when someone throws an old funnel cake away on the Jersey Shore boardwalk, messy and squawky. Each in their own time, they finished eating, and by finished eating, I mean threw more than half of their food away in the trash. The mothers would go to each of their respective daughters with what looked to be a tackle box, and pulled out creams and powders and hairspray and what not and re-touched their make up and re-puffed their very puffy bangs. The mothers, who smoked, smoked. The healthy mothers spent the extra few moments pep talking their daughters and crunching ice in their teeth.

When the last one of them left the dining area and the door closed, there was just me sitting in the corner booth, the brown-haired girl behind the counter and the two cooks in the back of the kitchen area. It was dead silent, no other guests, no radio, nothing on the grill or in the fryer, just absolute dead silence. I'm not sure, but I swear to God, I could hear my Blizzard melting into a Heath Bar flavored milkshake.

I'm not sure why this day had stuck out to me so much, I'm not sure why the details of what transpired are burned so crisply into my memory. I love ice cream. I mean my food choices that day where the farthest thing from healthy, a large Heath Blizzard, a large order of onion rings, and 20 packets of ketchup isn't the model of restraint or discretion. I didn't know any of these girls or their mothers. I'm sure they very well may have been some of the most kind and pleasant people in the entire world, had I ever had the chance to actually talk to them. It was just when they were all there together with the fierceness of competition pumping through their veins and the desire to be the best, or the skinniest, or the prettiest. It made it almost impossible to see anything other than that. It was the pressure that the mothers had placed upon the young girls, squeezing any bit of youthfulness out of them. It was how all of their speech patterns assimilated to sound like one another's, nasally and slow, like a high pitched bullfrog in very slow motion. What frustrated me is that there were dozens and dozens of other groups just like this making it to were ever they where going, to compete or showcase or try out or whatever to a bunch of grownups who will pick apart, judge, scrutinize, evaluate, comment, and give value to their existence. I don't know what made me more upset as I finished my last bite of the nearly completely melted ice cream treat, that there are platforms and forums where adults get together and judge the looks and style and abilities of children, that parents are willing to put their children through the emotional hell and torment of always being in a competition of some kind, or that these children will grow up someday and become parents of their own children and in some sick twisted way perpetuate an emotionally and mentally unhealthy culture of never being good enough. I screamed on the inside of my mind!!!! This is unbelievable! What the hell is wrong with these people?

I pushed myself out of the booth and placed my feet on the sticky white and red tiled floor, and walked over to the garbage can to throw away my trash. It was still as quiet as can be in the dining room, the workers were motionless like a mannequin display in a department store window. I walk up to the front of the restaurant where the exit doors are located, and as I passed the front counter by the register I stopped and stood there looking at the girl with brown hair who was just as kind and gentle as can be. She asks me if there is anything else she can get for me, I stood there in silence for a moment (which may as well have been an eternity), and said, "Can

I have a large ice water with extra lemon, extra ice?" She smiled, and turned away to a counter behind her that had one already made with a lid and straw in it. She handed it to me and said, "Have a nice day, but you had better hurry up, it looks like your bus is leaving."

Ghosts: Living by Myself in the Middle of the Woods

I don't believe in ghosts, but I like the idea of them.

I personally don't wish to be haunted, or live in a house that is haunted, but I'd like to know that there are places for people to go after they die, even if it's to the same places they've been their whole lives.

It's weird that I don't ever think about ghosts until it starts to get chilly out.

I feel weird sometimes after I see a scary movie.

Not that I think that anything is out there to get me.

But after I see something scary, something inside of me is always looking over my shoulder to see if there is something lurking about. Weird huh?

I was 19 when I first watched the Blair Witch Project.

I lived on a 40 acre lot in the middle of the Pennsylvania woods, in a small blue-sided cabin.

It was a time where VHS tapes were still a thing.

I had a TV/VCR combo unit on an end table that was sitting in the corner.

There was never much to do around there.

I didn't have many friends. I felt like a fish out of water. I didn't drive. I walked every where, even in the rain.

I worked a double shift at the restaurant that night and was exhausted.

It was dark outside, the leaves were on the ground, it was mid-October.

I was alone.

After my shower, I made a bag of microwaved popcorn, and put on my favorite pair of sweat pants, the ones I've had since middle school.

I poured Cherry Pepsi into the biggest cup I had.

I got under the blankets, after pushing in the VHS tape and pressing play.

I adjusted the volume with the remote control.

I watched the whole movie, all the way to the end.

By that time I was scared.

I was scared of ghosts.

I was scared of ghosts that I wasn't afraid of two hours ago before I watched the movie.

I wondered why?

I had to urinate after drinking all that Cherry Pepsi.

I was afraid to get up.

I thought maybe the cabin was haunted.

I urinated into the large cup that was once filled with Cherry Pepsi.

I set it on the floor next to the couch I was lying in.

I pressed the power button and turned off the TV.

It me took a while to fall asleep.

I was afraid.

I was afraid of something that I wasn't afraid of before.

Why does it work like that?

Giant Eagle

I shit my pants in the local grocery store recently.

I grabbed a cart and made a right past the photo lab, towards the produce section.

I felt like I had a bit of gas built up.

I made an effort to let it out, in a normal, typical, usual fashion.

To my dismay, more than just gas passed through.

I immediately abandoned my shopping cart.

As discreetly as I could, I waddled through the organic dry goods section, past the salad bar, and the rotisserie chickens to the bathrooms on the right where they keep the pickles and pre-packaged sliced bologna.

Upon my arrival to the stall, I noticed a grocery store employee sitting on the can.

He was talking on his phone.

He was in no way interested in hurrying up.

Five minutes later, which seemed like an eternity, he was finished.

I scowled at him as I shuffled into the stall.

There was water on the floor.

It was very unkempt.

It took me a while to clean myself up.

It was the worst.

I was embarrassed.

I walked out of the bathroom and out of the store.

I never returned.

Untitled #1

Things are changing.

And it's about time.

I realized today that I'm not afraid anymore.

I'm not afraid of anything anymore.

I'm not afraid of my thoughts.

I'm not afraid that those thoughts are going to make me sin.

I don't even believe in sin. So, I can't be afraid of it.

I'm not afraid of failure. I came from a place that was very low to the ground.

What would it mean to fail? I am alive.

I spent too many years trapped in fear, pretending I was somewhere else in my mind...faking it.

I'm not afraid anymore...of anything.

I'm not afraid of Hell, or going there.

It's not even something I think about anymore.

I think about going to Hell about as much as I think about the Tooth Fairy, which isn't very much.

I'm just not going to be afraid anymore.

I spent so much time being nervous, worrying that there was someone watching me, judging me.

I was a nervous wreck; I was a leaf on a tree, shaking.

I was a pool of tears all the time.

I was crippled, on the floor in my own urine soaked pants.

I'm just not afraid anymore: of God, or Hell, or sin.

I'm free, for the first time ever,

Like swimming to the top of the water for a fresh breath

of air.

I'm not afraid of anything anymore.

Not like I used to be. I was a mess.

I was in prison. I was a dog on a chain, tied to a tree in a grassless backyard, with no food, no water, and no shade from the ever beating sun.

But now I'm free to do anything I want to do, and free to feel any way I want to feel.

So, since I'm not afraid anymore, I'll just go ahead and be myself.

Maybe you can do the same.

All you need to do is leave your fear behind.

Childhood Memory #14

My parents used to have an old blue Buick. It was a rusty piece of shit.

But I guess that's none of my business.

The new cars during that time started to come out with automatic windows; we still had hand-cranks on ours.

It was the 80's. We were driving at night.

I was a kid, my head was out of the window as the summer air breathed on my face.

We hit a bump, and a piece of rust from the car splintered off of the car and flew into my eyeball.

The piece was small, maybe half the size of a red lentil, but it was big enough to let me know that something has gotten into my eye.

I began to cry. It hurt real bad. When we got home, my eye was red and puffy.

It was noticeable that something was lodged in my eye.

My parents didn't have health insurance for us. My Dad decided to try to fish it out.

My Dad is not a doctor, nor was he ever. He painted houses.

He took a pair of tweezers and tried to dislodge the metal from my eye.

I screamed in pain for close to an hour, as my Mother paced the floor with nervousness.

Eventually, after he couldn't seem to figure out how to do a home surgery on a child's fragile eyeball, and after much persuasion, my Mother convinced my Father to take me to the emergency room.

Reluctantly, he agreed.

We got into the car and drove the few short miles to the
ER to see the doctor. He immediately sends me to
another hospital to have surgery.

The doctor comes in and asks me a series of questions
about what happened. He then asks why didn't we go
straight to the hospital.

I explained my Dad took tweezers to my eye and tried to
fix it at home.

The doctor kindly explained how foolish of a decision
that was.

He explained to my Father that my vision was more
valuable than any amount of money or any hospital
bill.

He said the good news is that my eye will be spared.

He said that when my Dad used the tweezers on my
eyeball that he pushed the rust even further into my
eye, and nearly blinded me in my left eye.

Even though my Dad never perused a career as a medical
practitioner, he still pursued at-home surgeries and
home remedies for serious childhood injuries.

Which made me skeptical if he heard anything the eye
doctor said about the value of your children's safety.

I'm now in my 30's, and I have 20x20 vision.

I don't believe in miracles or angels, but something
special happened to me that day.

I don't know if I'll ever have children of my own,
however.

Stroller Culture

I see out of the corner of my eye this mother,

With a fancy jacket on,

With movie star sunglasses,

Big hair, and fake fingernails,

Hoping to be noticed as someone in her early 20's, but
wearing her late 30's poorly.

Using her elbows, she lazily pushes the baby stroller
along the sidewalk.

Her hands are occupied with a cigarette, a Starbucks
coffee, and her cell phone, which her eyes are glued
to.

Maybe she should have thought twice.

Maybe she should have thought twice about a lot of
things.

No Trespassing

I never understood the concept of "no trespassing."

I understand the concept of ownership.

I understand the concept of commerce and trade.

But I struggle with how one owns land.

Who owned it before you,

And who owned it before them,

And how did they get it?

If someone gives me an item that has been stolen,

Even if I'm not the one who stole it,

I am still the bearer of a stolen item.

Just because someone gifts you something that is stolen,

Doesn't mean it belongs to you.

The item in your keep is still stolen.

I was walking along the railroad tracks down by the
water's edge.

The train stopped next to me and the conductor asked
what I was doing.

I told him I was going for a walk.

He said that I was trespassing, and I wasn't permitted to
walk there.

With a puzzled look on my face, I said, " Trespassing?"

"Whose land am I trespassing on?" I thought out loud.

The conductor heard me think out loud, and he
responded with a sharp and direct answer, "This land
belongs to the railroad."

I asked, "Where did they get it from?"

He said, "None of your goddamn business."

I continued to walk in the same direction I was going previously.

I saw a dead deer.

And then I saw another dead deer.

And then I went to the sidewall behind an unmarked building to urinate.

I've been taking new vitamins so my urine was bright yellow, the color of a highlighter marker.

I remember what Woody Guthrie said about this land that you're standing on, don't belong to nobody else but you, it's yours to stand on as long as you're standing there.

I saw another dead deer; I turned around and went home. I had walked about 7 miles in total.

The Rapture

I walked into a cat fight.

There was hissing and hair flying.

There may have been 8-12 empty plastic cups on the
table.

The jukebox was very loud, so even if you weren't angry
you had to shout.

The argument was really only between two of them.

It never got physical; it was just a disagreement.

The one on the left had a face that was painted with
sweat.

The one on the right chewed his gum so fast, he easily
could have chipped a tooth.

They were arguing about the Rapture.

They were both Christians, so neither one of them used
curse words.

They would start their sentences with stabs like: " You
would be an idiot if you thought . . . "

They were talking about the future.

They were arguing about a definite thing that had not yet
happened.

This made my mind feel like exploding.

These are two people that I considered to be my friends.

I considered putting in my two-cents a number of times.

Each time I just ordered another beer.

After I finished each beer, all I could do is order another
one.

After this cycle continued about 8 times, my vision was
blurry.

My speech was slurred, even though I was just talking to myself under my breath.

I eventually chimed in.

I said, "You both are talking about the unwritten future, as if it has already happened. Doesn't that bother you?"

The Rapture conversation ended, and rightfully so.

Untitled #2

At a house show, it's loud. A cool breeze blows across the
cigarette littered porch.

Unkempt twenty-somethings drink the cheapest warm
beer tucked tightly into a beer holster.

There is an old gallon sized milk jug cut that was in half
and had written on it: "$5 for touring bands. If you
have money for beer, you have money for punk."

I laugh to myself.

I light a cigarette, and draw a large sip of gin from the
plastic bottle I have in my inner pocket.

Some attendees are sitting on the hood of their car
parked about 6 spots east of the front porch eating a
vegan pizza.

Typical banter ensues, "Hey dude, did you here that new
split that so and so just put out? That shit is tight."

Or you may hear, "What time does this thing actually
start? The flier says 7:30 but it's 8:15 and no one has
played yet."

Of the age spectrum, I'm on the older side of things being
31, but I don't feel a day over 17.

I feel exactly the same way I did back then, just fatter and
less interested in dressing the part.

My friend's band is playing second; they're a loud crusty
5 piece with a girl singer. That's really why I'm here.

I feel weird listening in on all of the conversations
happening around me, but not weird in a bad way,
just regular weird.

I feel lucky that punk has chosen me. It's kind of like in
Harry Potter when the sorting hat tells you what
house you belong to.

You can wish all you want not to be in Ravenclaw or

Huffelpuff, but if that's where you are supposed to go, then that's just your lot In life.

This "punk" isn't for everyone.

Lots of people try when they are young as a means to remove themselves from what their parents expect from them; some people just think it's cool.

But for me, a 31 year old man, sitting on a porch listening to local bands cover Youth of Today songs at 11:30 PM on a Tuesday night after the cops have already shown up twice, and the neighbors are out on the front lawn scowling and shaking their heads. This is my normal.

This is where I feel safe.

This is where I'm at home.

There is no growing up.

There is no getting over it.

There is no other option. This is the life that has chosen me, and I am so lucky to have it.

I am so lucky to still feel it in my blood and in my guts.

I'm so lucky to be alive . . . and I am alive.

Bus Stop

There's only three things that happen at the bus stop that is stationed across the street from my house.

Either people are getting off the bus and going to where they need to be getting to.

Or they are getting on the bus to arrive at either another bus stop, or arriving to the places that they had been daydreaming about all day.

Or they are running either up the hill or down the hill to catch the bus that they had just missed. It used to really bum me out when you would see people franticly running for the bus and they would just miss it by a few steps, because it was very uncertain when and if another bus would ever come along.

The bus system in Pittsburgh may be the absolute worst thing about this fair city. They are unreliable, often late, and go to very limited places. And to be honest, the cab situation is pretty bleak too.

When I was in college, I took the bus to school and to work every day. It wasn't awesome then either. I used to ride with the same people almost every day. They (for the most part) would always sit in the same seat that they sat in the day before, and the day before that, and probably months and years before that. Sometimes you would have the same bus driver for 6 months at a time; sometimes they would be only for a few days. This was before everyone had an iPod. Some people read books, some tried to catch a quick nap (which never really worked in their favor), and I'm convinced that some of those people just rode around on the never ending bus loop route, just so they didn't have to be inside of their house anymore.

I saw a fist fight on Greyhound bus in Nashville,

Tennessee between an old white security guard and a big black woman in her late twenties. He tried to escort her off the bus for talking too loud. She didn't want to go. He grabbed her arm. She stood up and beat the living shit out of the man. It all happened so quickly. It happened right in front of me, like a movie, or a magic trick. I knew something was happening; I knew it was a fight, but I didn't for sure know how or why. I didn't do or say anything. I just sat there, comatose, like a slug, like a giant pile of dog shit on the side of the sidewalk. A nearsighted single mother with thick glasses and a loud annoying voice all of her own, who didn't even see the altercation tried to get a list of signatures together to file a complaint against the Greyhound security guard. I'm guessing she wanted a free ride out of the deal. I promised to never take a Greyhound bus ever again, and as of now, I have kept that promise to myself.

I took a Mega Bus one time to Harrisburg to see a girl I was briefly interested in. It dropped me off in a shopping center parking lot. She picked me up in her father's car. It was a brief and forgettable dating experience; we never had sex, or even came close, not even once. On the bus trip back to Pittsburgh four crust punk kids with 2 dogs occupied the back seat of the bus. The dogs pissed and shit all over the place. The mess dripped down the steps and splashed the people on the bottom level of the double-decker bus. They were drinking warm malt liquor and smelled about as bad as you could even imagine. Shortly after that trip, I called the girl I was briefly interested in and told her that it wasn't working out. She cried. It was the first time I had ever broken-up with someone over the phone. We have never spoken since then, and I'm pretty sure she blocked me on the Internet. I've taken that same bus to the eastern side of the state quite a few times since then, and

I always look out the window to see if she's there so I can apologize for being cold, and standoffish. She's never there.

BULL SHIT PYRAMID SCHEME

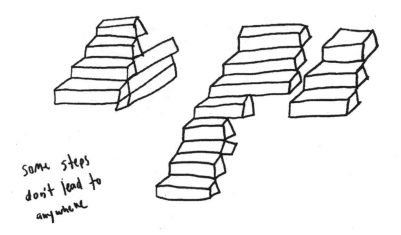

some steps
don't lead to
anywhere

Its ok
if you're
not going
any place at
all...
neither am I

It's nice to be Alone with someone who
who likes to be Alone as much as me.

A puppet show about a mountain called disappointment.

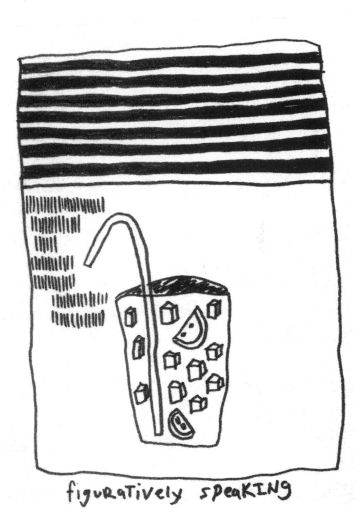

figuratively speaking

My parents house is a lot smaller than I remember.

Only the Appearance of Poverty.

Children Posing for a Fake Photo

Everyone is posing for some photograph somewhere

Whether they know it or not

It's interesting to think about how we all smile in our
   pictures

Even when we are sad

Even when the weight of it all seems to be resting on our
   very shoulders

There's a whole group of children taking self-portraits of
   themselves

In important seats

In front of important people

With their best friends

All smiling even though they aren't all feeling like smiling

Wearing clothes that they themselves can't afford to be
   wearing

With a cell phone that they didn't pay for

There is something horribly wrong when we feel like
   everything has to be so great all the time

When the smiles in our pictures aren't real

When its hard to know what is real and what's not

Sometimes I think about what it would be like if we
   began to take pictures of ourselves when we are sad,
   when we cry, when we feel ugly with snot running
   down our faces

When we begin to tell the truth about ourselves

And stop pretending

Pretending like every moment is the best

And moments can just be moments

Instead of posing for pictures

That people only envy

While they are wondering

Why they feel so lonely and everyone else is smiling all
the time?

Clouds

After we had sex for the first and only time,

There was a noticeable black cloud that followed me
around for the months to come.

It reminded me of how bad my teeth hurt.

It made me slouch when I sat down.

It made my eyelids awkwardly heavy all the time.

Like my heart was pumping molasses or peanut butter.

My hands where always clammy. I smelled like an
abandoned church.

Everything tasted either bland or too salty.

I had dreams of myself being followed by this black
cloud.

In those dreams, I was always talking to someone on a
landline telephone

With a spiraled telephone cord, that seemingly went on
forever.

I always was wearing corduroy pants one size too small
that hurt my waistline.

I could never walk fast enough to avoid the big black
cloud.

It was like trying to run barefoot on the beach, not easy.

I had that drunken night stained in my mind.

I had nightmares that she had gotten pregnant.

Years later, she would show up on my door step with a
kid that looks like me,

But with a name that I never would have chosen like
Scott, or Bret, or Clayton.

The kid had a black cloud following him too.

He looked sad.

I'm sure he hated me.

He asked me if I was his dad.

I said, "I think so."

I asked him what he thought of that.

He just shrugged.

His mother was dropping him off to live with me for now on.

He only had a small bag of clothes.

I asked him if he liked grilled cheese.

He said, "I'm gluten free."

I said, "Me too."

He smiled.

She left and both of our black clouds left with her.

We went inside, out of the cold, and listened to the Beatles on vinyl and ate our gluten-free grilled cheese sandwiches.

Sometimes, I would dream the whole dream, but most times, the dream would end with her on my front porch with the young boy, and me in the doorway in tight corduroy pants.

Doing Nothing

All those years in high school

working so hard

getting good grades,

all those letters of recommendation,

all those college applications,

getting accepted to your first three choices.

Grandpa gave you the old Dodge Stratus to take off to school with you. Grandma made you a quilted blanket that matches with the corresponding school colors.

Mom and Dad were so proud that day when you left and went off to school.

Met a girl the first few weeks of freshman year, and quickly fell in love.

We went to 1000 parties together, drank beer together, went on double dates.

We switched holidays with each other's parents every year. We became best friends. Junior year we got engaged. It's hard to find someone loyal now-a-days. I found someone loyal, maybe it's just luck.

We got married the following summer after graduation.

I got that job that I really wanted.

40- 55 hours a week. Rush hour both ways.

You gotta keep your eye on the bottom line, so you can hold it all together.

With a little saving and planning we bought our first house. It didn't need much work. We picked out all the furniture and decorations.

We always got a real Christmas tree. The needles hide out until late spring.

About 3 years after that, we had our first kid.

18th months later, we had another.

We have good health care.

She stays at home with the kids, cooks, cleans, smiles when I come home.

This cycle goes on for about the next 5 years or so.

We bought an SUV. That's nice. We are still paying off our mortgage, and will for quite a bit longer, I assume.

Yesterday was my 28th Birthday. I feel nice. Life is nice, wife is nice, kids are nice.

Never any surprises, never a bump in the road. We go to the movies regularly. We still have dinner as a family as often as possible.

Things are normal, things are safe, things are miserable.

Early Morning Watching Videos about Arnold Schwarzenegger

I spent a good piece of early morning (from about 5:45 AM to 6:30 AM) watching videos of Arnold Schwarzenegger in his twenties when he was the world's top bodybuilding champion. He was smiling and helping other weightlifters get bigger and stronger. He was a popular guy; people liked him. He was young, and attractive. He had women throwing themselves at him, like leaves through a chain link fence. People would line up around the corner like at a bread line or a funeral precession to see him flexing, to get a glimpse of the bulgy handsome, well put together, funny talking man with beautiful eyes and tan skin. His fellow bodybuilders would ogle over him from the minute he walked into the gym, until after he got in his car and drove away. He had a nice head of hair. It was full and brown, and he didn't wear a mustache like some other bodybuilders did during that time period that just made them look creepy and awkward. His movie career was about to really take off, and even though (in my humble opinion) he was a pretty lousy actor, people seemed to really like him. He often referred to his life as a never-ending orgasm. He always felt good. Whether he was in the gym or he was with a woman, or in front of a camera, he always felt like he was at the top of the world. And it's so true that nothing lasts forever.

Her Time was Well Spent

There's no telling how long we have until it's all over, until our heart gives out or our brains stop telling the rest of our body how to go.

We all have an invisible hourglass hanging over our heads, that keeps us suspended in this maze we call being alive.

The amount of time left for Joanna is as uncertain as anyone else, I suppose.

She hasn't a clue when her last day will be.

She was told it was supposed to be years ago, when she was much younger than she is now, because of a brain tumor that she carries.

But every day she wakes up, and smiles, and gets to be alive.

She is holding on to her late 20's with cotton ball fingertips and faithful wonderment.

With jogging shoes, and yoga pants, and organic grocery lists written in longhand cursive, Direct Trade Guatemalan pour-over coffee, a tooth brush made out of old melted recycled water bottles, a hand me down Stevie Nicks twirly skits that reminds me of how much I HATE Fleetwood Mac. She sits on my front porch with a glass of anything as she tells me how much today counts, and that if I didn't go out and do exactly what I wanted to do today that one day I may live to regret it . . . or even worse that I may not.

Time is precious.

We don't have a lot of it.

This could literally be the end of the line for you, or me, or your brother, or your Great Aunt Susan.

So you gotta make it count.

You gotta at least try your best to get out there and see
something.

Don't play it safe.

Don't listen to what someone else tells you is best for
your life.

Joanna certainly isn't. She lives on a bus, and travels, and
feels things with her skin. And has original thoughts
in her mind, and wears kindness like a summer dress.

She wrote me a letter in my dream one time when we
were at a picnic under a tree. A multitude of our
friends were there laughing, and drinking, and eating,
sharing in the shade that the tree provided. And you
were there, and you were there, and you were there,
and you were there.

The note read: knowing that today is just today and
tomorrow is as uncertain as uncertainty. Tomorrow
is something we all have had handed to us in very
different ways whether we are dead or alive.

She could die today from a tumor that lives on her brain,
but she doesn't ever spend too much time thinking
about that. She's too busy being free.

She stepped out of the car and onto the oil spill stained parking lot in her teal colored flip-flops, toenails painted pink, wearing a warm smile, and said (after a long inhale) "It smells like New Hampshire here." She always wore her hair in a ponytail. Her jeans always had a hole in the knee. She carried around thankfulness in her backpack, so she wouldn't go anywhere without it. Her smile was the brightest light; her heart was always on her sleeve. She had great faith in humanity, loved to hold babies, and baby kittens. She had great posture; her shoulder blades were sharp and would often poke out of the back of her tank-top during the summer months. Every Saturday after lunch, she would smoke two cigarettes consecutively, to remind her that it's okay to enjoy things from time to time, but not to allow yourself to become owned by them.

Her teeth were white as snow, but carried a crooked bend to them that made her that much more human, that much more kind looking. She sang in the shower an old Judy Garland tune, that you can hear from the furnace returns that sounded like an angel's choir. Sometimes she would tell me things about my grandmother and how much she loves me, that she would pray for me, that she still prays for me now but in a much different way. She would tell me that my grandmother is close to me still even though she has been gone now for quite some time. That love can build a bridge that can gap to even the most lonely and sad hearts. That I shouldn't give up. That my grandmother was so proud that I made it this far, even though it didn't always see it that way.

She began to tell me about herself. She was born an accident, like a car crash, like a bad note on an out of tune piano. She was born in a bad house with bad parents with little chance in life, or little hope of ever making it. She had been beaten down and forgotten about, the voices that used to speak to her were harsh and smelled of regret, but she made it this far. With gratitude in her heart, with a paycheck called experience that can't get spent, or cashed in, by anyone else, she made it. She made it this far.

Honesty on the Train

From Pittsburgh to New York City is about a 9-hour trip via the train. I have a window seat per usual. It's sunny and very clear out. The attendant for today's trip, Ray, said it's going to be a full one, so don't place bags or items on the seat next to you as to keep all seats open for future passengers. He is very pleasant, and looks to be about my age, perhaps a few years my senior. He has a warm smile, and a very soft and friendly voice. One can never be sure, but I'm confident that he enjoys his job. As he came past to check my ticket, he tells me that the café will open shortly for breakfast. I ask him for a garbage bag for the pretzels that I spilled all over the floor about two minutes after I was seated. He said he didn't have one. So, I kicked them to the side and hid them under my backpack. A nervous white boy sat next to me about half way through the trip. His mother and father sat in front of him. He didn't say one word to me as he sat there, which I was fine with. I wonder why he was nervous; I wonder if he noticed the pretzels spilled all over the floor under my backpack. As soon as another seat opened up, he darted for it. When he got there, he put his head in his hands and wept. His parents didn't try to comfort him; they just looked embarrassed. I went to the trolley café and bought 2 Cherry Pepsis. I handed him one, and I kept one. He took it and said thanks. It's weird to feel feelings.

June 8, 2014

I don't go to church anymore, for many reasons. However, I have been thinking a lot about how it all makes me feel. It's good to remind yourself sometimes of what you don't want to do, what you don't want to turn into, what you want to avoid. I think about the terrifying feeling I get from driving up to the parking lot of the mall in my hometown. It's almost crippling, like a deer caught in the headlights. Paralyzed.

I never buy anything; I just walk around with my sunglasses on desperately trying to feel nothing. Trying not to become ill after smelling all the different colognes and perfumes from the old ladies with their tan leather faces, wearing a feathered boa at the salad bar, lipstick on their teeth, alone with all their friends, sharing their fading memories.

I feel the same way about going to church as I imagine I would feel in the Mall of America. Overstimulated, like a sales pitch, like an advertisement, like a billboard museum. Once my bottom touches the pew, I feel like I'm covered with a hot wet mayonnaise soaked blanket, covered in cat hair. I don't feel good. Maybe it's the devil inside of me trying to get out. Maybe it's everything else. I just know it's the same feeling as going to a children's birthday party at McDonald's or Chucky Cheese, disgusted. I just feel awkward, but yet, I still find myself going to church about 3 times a year, just so I can know what it's like to feel that feeling, just so I know what I should avoid.

Some people love going to church, they love the feeling they get from it, they love the goose bumps, they love guilt leaving their body. And then some people love going to the dentist. I don't understand that either.

Legs

Today, I decided to go to the food court in a mall by my parents' house, to get Chinese food from the Amazing Wok Lunch Buffet. It had all the typical items you would expect: General Tso's chicken, crab rangoon, beef with broccoli, hot and sour soup, fried rice, and those little fried doughnut desserts that are covered in granulated sugar. The lighting was dim, the food was just warm enough to not be cold. It had a grey flavor to it. The soy sauce tasted like it was watered down.

There was a fellow in the corner well in into his 50's sitting in a booth with a girl half his age that he was treating to a lunch date. The man sounded just like Jell-O Biafra from the Dead Kennedys, which caught my attention. He was going on about all of his accomplishments. The girl wasn't impressed. I felt like a fish out of water, like I was breathing in heavy air. The lighting was bad, and the décor on the walls looked like they came from a dollar store in Chinatown.

Just then, I see a man by himself, without any legs, in a wheelchair rolling his way up to the buffet. He looked around at the different items in the stainless-steel steam table rolling back and fourth in-between the two wood paneled serving islands. He pushed himself away from the buffet, went back to his table gathered his belongings and began to leave the restaurant without ever taking a bite to eat. When Mr. Kim (the owner) asked him if there was something wrong, he simply replied, "Well, you can't please everyone I guess" and rolled his way out of the restaurant.

Manhattan in August: Pizza Shop Blues

LED lights in uncountable numbers, with a blinding fury scream for attention as the passers by walk amused in a sleepless dance from bar to bar and shop to shop. The trash is piled higher than most cars parked along the curbs of 25th and 3rd. I've never seen so many people at the end of their rope. Immigrants smoking cigarettes well past the filter. The boys are all wearing salmon colored denim shorts, with backward snapback baseball hats, every word they said sounded like they where just saying "Snapple, Snapple, Snapple, Snapple" over and over again. There is an Asian woman jogging laps around this particular block in a skirt, wearing her salt and peppered hair like a crown; her glasses slide down her sweat soaked nose. The fire hydrant is open, spraying water on the oncoming traffic, one car had their window open and soaked the whole back seat of girls who looked like they were dressed to have dinner with Vampire Weekend. They didn't see the water spraying, because they were all on their cell phones, wishing they were somewhere else.

I looked to my left towards the corner where the most wonderful Monday night pizza smell with a cheap beer special was wafting through the air like sheets drying in the wind. I looked through the advertisements past the window inside of the middle of the central table section to see a man sitting at a 4-chaired table by himself. He had two empty beer bottles pushed to the far side of the table past the red pepper flakes and parmesan cheese, both of which he probably didn't touch, and a Coke with no ice to his immediate reach. The sweat from the paper Coke cup had gathered in a circle on the table as to show he had been there for quite some time. He slowly cut his pizza into bite-sized pieces with his disposable plastic cutlery and slowly chewed each bite for what seemed to be anywhere from 28-32 times. After each bite he would wipe the sides of his mouth with a paper napkin even though there was no pizza residue to clean off. All around him were couples on dates laughing and joking and drinking and making eyes at one another. At the far west end of the room was a table full of college-aged athletic types guzzling beer and talking about how much pussy they've gotten as of recently. When the solo flying man heard one of their jokes he would throw his head back in laughter, pretending like he was a part of the joke. His shirt was neatly ironed. His pants pleated, his hair so neatly parted. He lived in a one-bedroom apartment. He had one cup in his cupboard, one fork, one spoon, one butter knife, and he kept them neatly lined up on a paper towel on his kitchen counter. He had a maid, and a laundry service; he had a driver to take him to and from work. He had a garage with one car parked in it that he hardly ever used. He had a goldfish named Buddy that he fed every morning at 5:15 AM. He was fit and well put together; He had plenty of money, and plenty of time to think, took vacation by himself every February to Maui. All he wanted was someone to share it with, but never knew how to be anything other that what he was told to be, which often left him feeling lonesome.

One Small Answer about Me

I read an article on some newsfeed the other morning, while I was drinking my morning coffee at my dining room table. The headline read like a gunshot, like a mega phone, like it was written to envelop my attention. It read: "Do you ever wonder how you get your bad behaviors?" It was just what I was looking for. It was an answer to what was hunting me down, like a pack of wolves with the scent of fresh blood in the air. I needed to know why I felt so weird all the time. I wanted to blame my inconsistent mood on something. I wanted to know why I got so angry sometimes. I wanted to know why loneliness felt like I was dying, and how I could never sever the ropes that tied me to the tracks of my mental instability.

I took the first sip of my coffee, and got past the heading of the article, and this is what I learned about everything:

In a test lab somewhere in New England, a study was being done on about how fear and anger is transferred generation to generation through DNA. That not only do you get your mother's nose, your father's eyes and your great-grandfather's freckle pattern, but you also get their bad temper, addictive personality, and even their fears. So often we think that behaviors are learned and embedded through a routine of examples, but what if there is something in your blood that makes you predisposed to certain feelings, like fear, anger, addiction, or even poverty. That maybe you never had to meet your crackhead dad, or your hotheaded mother to receive their ill temperament or addictive personalities.

A mouse was tested for 30 days in a controlled environment with a series of basic tests to prove that fear can be transferred though blood genetically. For 30 days scientists would feed a mouse a very small piece of cheese at the start of a maze followed by placing a lavender plant in between the mouse and a larger piece of cheese on the other end of the maze. After the mouse would eat the small piece of cheese it would begin to travel towards the lavender plant to get towards the larger piece of cheese. Whenever the mouse would get up to the lavender plant to cross over to get to the larger piece of cheese, it would receive a shock by a small probe attached to the lavender plant. With every time the mouse would try to brave the journey across the lavender plant, the shock value would get stronger and stronger, to the point where the mouse quit trying to go near the lavender plant.

After about 15 days, the mouse would eat the small piece of cheese, and instead of trying to go close to the lavender, it would just lay down and give up. The scientists rerouted the maze to start the mouse with the lavender being at the beginning and forcing the mouse to go past it to get the cheese. The scientists took down the electric probe and didn't shock the mouse when it came around the lavender. And even though the mouse knew that there was no shock when it passes by the lavender' its heart rate would still grow fast and show the same signs of fear that it did when it received the shock. The mouse would often just lay down at the beginning of the maze and not pursue the cheese, even when it was starving, because the fear had paralyzed the mouse.

On the 30th day of testing, the scientists removed semen from the mouse and impregnated a female mouse with the male's seed. Moments before extracting the semen from the male mouse, it was dropped in a maze that was filled only with lavender, every direction, every step the mouse was faced with lavender. The mouse was panicked, fearful, and uneasy. As soon as the scientists knew that the pregnancy had took, the male mouse was put to death. The female mouse had gone full-term and delivered offspring. The new born mice where fed regularly, offered care, love, clean and luxurious amenities (for mouse standards), and was fed delicious imported cheese on a regular basis.

When the mice were old enough to be recognized as adolescent, they were placed in a maze with ten doors. Behind each door was a small piece of cheese with an obstacle standing in front of it: a Lego, a thimble, a q-tip, so on and so on. The mouse would bypass the obstacle with great ease and enjoy the small delicious cheese. This went on for the first 9 doors. However, on the tenth door the obstacle that was in front of the cheese was a few small lavender leaves, the mouse walked up to the door, and when it opened and saw the lavender, it was immediately filled with fear, anxiety, and showed great signs of stress. The mouse slowly backed up and refused to pursue the final piece of cheese. This mouse was never exposed to lavender before in its life, had never been shocked, nor had ever even met its father to know anything about him, and his traumatic experiences with lavender. There was something deep inside the mouse that gave it a predisposed fear of lavender. There was a very present and real sense of fear that swept over the mouse that was unfounded, and not based within the confines of its own experiences, which makes me think about my own behaviors. There are things in my life that I can't explain. There are behaviors that I have to fight against every day that I have no clue where they came from.

My one friend Chris never met his dad, he was killed in a car crash by a drunk driver on his way home from work when his mother was 7 months pregnant. Chris looks like his dad, he has is chin, and teeth, and Chris's mother swears that their feet are identical. But one thing that I find to be remarkable is that Chris has a very unique laugh, it's like a deep belly laugh that is as contagious as poison ivy or the hiccups. He never met his dad, never heard him speak, cry, or laugh. Last year Chris's mom died of a brain aneurism, and Chris was willed all of her belongings. Among the belongings was a VHS tape of Chris's dad at a holiday party. Chris saw a video of his dad for the first time, heard his voice for the first time, and heard his laugh for the first time. It was the exact the same laugh as his. Chris is 31. I think this explains a lot, about everything I have ever wondered about myself. I'm not so hard on myself anymore. It's kind of nice.

Miley Cyrus

Why do some people get such great satisfaction out of telling others that their art sucks? I was sitting there in my dining room with a piece of cake and a glass of almond milk reading the comments that some people were making about this dance that Miley Cyrus did at some big fancy corporate music award ceremony. Some people grew to be so angry with her that they thought maybe the world would be better off if she had killed her self. They used words like "whore," and "slut," and "waste of space." Now, I don't know much about this girl. I know she's famous. I know her dad wrote some country tunes in the early 90's. I think she was in some way related to the Disney Channel, but I know nothing more than that. I think it's safe to say that I know more about her than she knows about me.

I also can be honest when I say that I don't particularly care for the art that she makes, not to say that it is bad, or that no one should like it, or that I think she should kill herself. I simply prefer to listen other music, when I have the time to do so. It's so easy to put somebody down, especially when we don't have to look them in the face. I wish that type of behavior would go away.

(Pain Killers)   Harmony Korine Short Story Workshop: We Co-Wrote This Story

When I was in middle school, I can remember a girl who tried to kill herself by eating a bottle of painkillers. Her younger sister found her, and she got her stomach pumped at a hospital. There was damage to her liver that would last her the rest of her life. She was in a bad car accident when she was a little girl, which made her walk with a limp. I don't think she knew her real dad, but her mother always had a new boyfriend every six months. So, I'm sure that helped. Her mother did wind up getting remarried to a guy named Andy years later, who she drove crazy, and he drove his car into the cinderblock wall of a Blockbuster Video at 100 miles an hour. He died instantly; the coroner said he was sober.

My mom said that that girl just wanted to be noticed, that she actually didn't want to die; she just didn't know of any other way to get attention. I always thought that it must have been a sad environment to grow up in. This girl had two other sisters both younger than she. I believe they all got pregnant before High School graduation. It's always been interesting to think about what people will do to get attention from someone else. For sure her mother was crazy, I think her first husband killed himself too. Her mother made and sold crafts at the flea market behind the old horse track. I think that was where her daughter bought the painkillers she took as a means to kill herself; I mean get attention.

Okay

Some people only ask how you are doing to hear the
   word "okay."

They don't really care, they just don't want to feel
   responsible when you eventually lose your mind and
   try to hurt yourself.

They say things like: "Yeah man, I mean I asked him how
   he was doing. He always seemed to be okay."

Okay like a jackhammer drill bit going through your front
   two teeth.

Okay like a divorce court.

Okay like almost spoiled milk.

Okay like surviving suicide.

Sometimes, I wish they would ask a different question.
   Sometimes, I wish I had answered with an honest
   answer.

Untitled #3

Somewhere in the middle of average is where most things go to die. For some, it's not a far journey. They've been living there all of their lives, but could never recognize it. It's very room temperature there, very reachable, and nothing has flavor. No one is ever hungry there, nor are they full, which isn't to be mistaken with contentment. Most who live here are very gullible and are easily tricked, bamboozled, or hoodwinked. When they are asked about the kind of music they like, their response is usually something like, "Uh . . . I don't know. Whatever's on the radio I suppose."

Everything feels rushed all the time, but no one is ever going anywhere, like the blurry lines between indifference and comfort. There are a million pills everywhere to make you feel different, but the longer you take them, the less they actually work, like a placebo effect, like losing your innocence, like the Reagan Administration. Everything is always in need of a dusting, and all the apples are mealy in consistency. The magazines are a constant reminder of just how average everything is supposed to be, and most of your day is spent merely being distracted. Everyone is able to see what is wrong with everyone else around them, but can see nothing wrong with the blank emptiness of their own selves.

The Understanding of Reasonable Loyalty

I have been betrayed very few times in my life.

My close friends are very loyal and true. So, I guess that makes me lucky.

So when I do get betrayed, it hurts real bad.

Even when I get slighted, it hurts real bad.

I like people, and I like it when people like me,

Even to a fault.

I want people to like me more, almost more than anything else.

My feelings get hurt easily if I feel ignored or left out.

I'm a hugger; I'm a great hugger.

I like to grab the back of peoples' shirts when I hug them and grip it tightly into my fist and pull hard on it.

Sometimes, if I'm really close with someone, I'll bury my nose into their neck and just hold it there until the feeling passes.

I think I'm a loyal friend.

I guess I just don't want to feel like I can be easily replaced.

I want to be an irreplaceable friend.

I'm fine with being an average artist.

I'm fine with being a forgettable writer.

I'm not fine with being a replaceable friend.

I guess if I were to say I had a phobia, this would be it.

Things I'm Afraid of

I've only been afraid of two basements in my life: my grandparents', and the basement in the house that I grew up in. My grandparents' basement had way too many doors for a normal basement, and the sight of it terrified me. My parents' basement was unfinished for most of my life, dirt floors, spiders, cobwebs, wet, cold etc. etc. etc. One time my Dad sent me downstairs to find an old oil paint brush for him in the back corner of the farthest room, and when I was all the way down there in the far corner, he shut the lights off. I've never been the same.

When Jack Grows Up

A dad looks down at his son (age 5) wearing his Buzz Lightyear pajamas.

His son looks him in the eyes and says, "Hey Dad, what are you going to be when you grow up?"

His dad says, "I'm going to be a dad."

"What are you going to be when you grow up son?"

He says, "Either a dinosaur or Buzz Lightyear."

Dad says, "That sounds like a great deal."

"Do you think there going to need for a new Buzz Lightyear by the time you grow up?"

Son says, "Yeah, of course. By the time I grow up, it will time to get a new Buzz."

"Well, what else do you want to be if you can't get a job being Buzz or a dinosaur?"

"I don't know. What would you want me to be dad?"

Dad says, "Anything, anything in the whole wide world, except for a cop or a soldier."

Son says , "Okay, I'll just stick with being Buzz."

Wizard of OZ

There's this movie that is always playing in my head.

It switches back and forth between color and black and
   white,

Just like the Wizard of OZ.

It also has a man behind the curtain just like the Wizard
   of OZ.

It plays like a daydream,

Or the feeling that exists in between sober and not sober
   anymore.

His voice will come over everything like a loud speaker,
   like a car alarm, like the police beating a guy, like fear.

The same sentences are on loop for sometimes hours at a
   time.

From the moment I stepped off the train, until the
   moment I decided to leave three days later,

This is what I heard on repeat,

like a mantra being chanted by an alienating chorus:

"Every block in midtown Manhattan smells like a
   different scent of piss.

In the summer its almost unbearable, kind of like the
   news of terminal cancer.

It's like the sewers can't hold it all, and it seeps up
   through the cracks in the pavement."

It's no shock that there are homeless people everywhere
   here.

It's rough to keep your wits about you.

Everyone is guilty of something it seems.

Either they are trapped in here against their will, or they
   were sold an illusion that doesn't exist.

Look around at the competition.

Everyone is sizing you up,

Like boxers before a fight,

Like the wild dogs in the zoo that ate the kid who fell in,

Like sharks in blood infested waters,

Like it's like Black Friday everyday,

The rush, the hustle, the sweat, the worry, the anxiety.

It's like the feeling of the first few minutes of high school,
but that feeling lasts forever,

Like being bullied by someone you used to call a friend.

Nothing good is familiar.

We are out to get you.

You are all alone.

It's everywhere you look, in the stores, in the restaurants,
walking down the street with short shorts and
sunglasses.

And who the fuck do you think you are in the mix of it all?

Memories

I don't remember breast feeding, but I'm told it was a huge part of my past. I still have dreams about losing my teeth. I can remember that feeling. I can taste the blood in my mouth, the pop sound when the tooth departs from the socket it broke away from. I can still feel the tooth swimming around in my mouth like a hard skinned gold fish. I can remember feeling lost in a flea market, when I was separated from my grandfather in a place where a used car lot auction now stands. I can remember watching grown-ups cry at a funeral for people they never met. I often wondered why they cried, but now I think I get it. I can remember my great grandmother's mustache and wondered how things like that happened. I can remember not knowing the difference between poor and rich. I can remember my first vinyl record album; it was Alvin and the Chipmunks Christmas record. I can remember sitting in a stroller at a park with my mom in Clariton, Pennsylvania, there was a water fountain, there was a lunch cart. We ate a ham sandwich. I can remember when my He-Man toys where taken away from me because the minister told my parents that the devil was in the plastic. I remember crying about that. I can remember trick or treating when I was 4 years old, in the rain, as a clown, walking through the puddles with my Velcro shoes, in the neighborhood surrounding my parent's house, with my little brother and my best friend from down the street. I remember sitting on Santa's lap at the Century 3 Mall outside of Horn's. Some kids spent hours in line, only to cry when it was their turn. I still don't understand why they did that. I remember the first time I heard about divorce. It made me sad, even though you get two birthday parties, and two Christmases. Two parents that stuck it out would be a lot better, or so I thought at the time. I'm not so sure about that anymore.

I remember going downtown and seeing the abortion signs with the dead babies on it. Sometimes, when I have a really bad dream I'll see flashes of that day right before I wake up. I remember one time in 1989, a kid in a high chair had diarrhea so bad that it squirted out of his diaper and onto the floor. I couldn't eat anything with Swiss cheese on it for like 15 years after that. I remember catching my first fish in a stream in Ligonier, Pennsylvania. I can remember when my brother almost choked to death on a corned beef sandwich, and his face turned blue and his eyes rolled into the back of his head. I can remember my first haircut. (I was about 3.) It was at a Vo-tech school that I would later attend when I was in 11th grade. I can remember my first sip of beer. It was Stoney's light from a can in my grandparents' garage. I can remember listening to AC/DC at a party at my aunt's house when I was about 6 and my parents telling me that it was Devil music. I can remember watching The Lion, the Witch and the Wardrobe (the BBC cartoon version) every day on VHS cassette tape for about 4 years. I remember having a Teddy Ruxpin doll that had a short circuit and would randomly turn on and start taking in the middle of the night. I didn't know what demon possession was at that time, but if I did, I surely would have blamed it on that. I can remember getting a piece of rust from an old Buick lodged in my eyeball one summer. I still have 20/20 vision. I can remember my parents' waterbed. It smelled like a brand new tennis ball. I can remember the first time I was afraid of losing my mind. I was about 7 years old when I went to my grandmother's house in Mckeesport where I played with Play-Doh in a dimly lit room filled with cigarette smoke and dog hair. She wore red lipstick on her teeth, and drank warm buttermilk with salt and pepper. She often cried. She said her memory was fuzzy; sometimes my memory is fuzzy   too.

The End of It: I Hope You Understand

It's not your fault that things turned out this way.

You were so young when it all happened to you.

It was like a rushing wave, of everything, that made you
feel like nothing.

It's the emptiness that keeps us apart.

It's the vacancies of the things we are told have value that
drag us down.

It's not your fault.

You were told it wouldn't turn out like this,

That you would be okay,

That time was on your side. Tell that to the cemetery.
Tell that to the cigarette salesman.

This life is but a vapor, but a flash. As soon as you get
going, it's over.

Be awesome to each other.

Be kind. Be generous.

Smile.

Don't bully people to do what you want them to do.

And don't let people get bullied.

Don't sign up for war; it will kill you.

Take your time, and love everything the best you can.

Bad breath is a part of life, don't let it bum you out.

Drink plenty of water. Watch your sugar intake.

Get shoes with good arch support.

Don't let the hipsters make you feel bad for being
yourself.

Fall in love with whoever you want to,

Whoever loves you back.

Don't let some church push you around, be your own person.

Don't start smoking cigarettes. It's a huge waste of time and money.

If someone tells you to grow up, tell them no way José.

Be kind.

Smile.

I'm proud of you.

My name is Derek Zanetti. I am currently 32 years old. I live in Pittsburgh, Pennsylvania. I have a dog. I travel, make music, write stories and make art. I try to never do anything that I don't want to do.

Made in the USA
Charleston, SC
08 December 2015